A souvenir guide

Charlecote Park
Warwickshire

Siân Evans

National Trust

Charlecote remembered

by Sir Edmund Fairfax-Lucy

Above Sir Edmund's father,
Sir Brian Fairfax-Lucy

Opposite The Stables

Few now remember Charlecote as a private house.

In the 1960s my father, Brian, wrote that the entertainment he loved best was to watch the comings and goings of the tradesmen's carts and to feed the horses from a dish of washed carrots after their manes had been plaited on Sundays.

'To escape the watchful eyes of our elders, we would wake early and go out of the house, taking down the heavy bars on the doors before it was light and before anyone was about, just to explore the unknown, to find moorhens' nests or climb trees, or walk along the ridges of the roof.'

I still find it a great thrill, arriving at Charlecote at dusk to see its imposing skyline unchanged, just as it was when the roofs sheltered twenty people and as many horses. I find it a comfort to think that, even with no trace of medieval Charlecote visible, there are still herons fishing along the banks of the Avon; and that we hear the barking of the deer coming through the mist. You see a collection from seven generations. Three more have to worry how something of this scale can continue.

'In 1939', Brian wrote, 'I thought Charlecote could not survive another war, the blinds were drawn, the staff reduced, many lovely trees had been cut down to allow bombers to fly into a nearby airfield and from one view it looked like a stag that had lost an antler.... When I visited Charlecote after the National Trust had acquired it and mingled with visitors, I realised how great a heritage it was, but I longed to show them, "here I caught my first fish, there is the garden that I dug or, that I was only seven when I climbed to the top of the great cedar tree." Inside, I looked at the pictures of my ancestors in the Great Hall, which seemed strangely bleak without its log fire, which we had delighted to poke to see the sparks fly up the black chimney. I thought the Library now seemed cold and empty. The little ornaments that I had fondled and cherished had disappeared, so too the easy chairs, the piles of unanswered letters and the half-finished trays of tea, so I crept back to where once I had watched the horses and carriages arrive and I could still picture myself leaning out through the bars. I sat and pondered.... Charlecote had emerged unaltered in its character still basking in its tranquil surroundings.'

Those who wrought this have gone, but surely they would be astonished and delighted that the Past has been put at the service of the Present, that a family lives here and everything is so lovingly kept.

Welcome to Charlecote

'It is a most delightful place. All about the house and domain there is a perfection of comfort and domestic taste, an amplitude of convenience, which could have been brought about only by the slow ingenuity and labour of many successive generations.... One man's lifetime is not enough for the accomplishment of such a work of Art and Nature.'

Nathaniel Hawthorne, American writer and traveller, 1863

Set in a beautiful park in the heart of England, Charlecote Park seems to embody the Golden Age of the first Queen Elizabeth.

The ancient Warwickshire countryside has a timeless quality with its meandering waterways, venerable trees, wildlife and waterfowl. Fallow deer crop the lush grass along the banks of the River Avon, which flows through the park and on to Stratford-upon-Avon some five miles away.

Son of Stratford

The most famous son of Stratford, William Shakespeare, risked a promising career here, when at the age of 19 and recently married, he was allegedly caught poaching from Sir Thomas Lucy I's Fulbrook property, which adjoins Charlecote. He was punished by the landowner and ran off to London, but had his revenge in later years by parodying Sir Thomas as Justice Shallow in *The Merry Wives of Windsor*. It was the link to Shakespeare which persuaded the National Trust to take on the estate in 1946, and the connection survives to the present day.

A royal visitor

One illustrious visitor received a royal reception at Charlecote. In August 1572 Queen Elizabeth stayed here after visiting nearby Kenilworth where she had been entertained by her favourite, Robert Dudley, Earl of Leicester. She is said to have occupied the Great Bedchamber on the ground floor where the Drawing Room now stands.

A passion for nostalgia

It was this historic visit which prompted a later generation of the Lucy family to create a romantic vision of the house in the reign of 'Good Queen Bess'. They refitted the principal rooms in Elizabethan Revival style, filling them with treasures, such as an extensive collection of paintings, and adding to a wonderful library of rare books. Once criticised as a revivalist fake, the house and its magnificent contents provide a unique insight into the nineteenth century's passion for nostalgia.

The continuous thread which runs through the Charlecote story is the Lucy family, who have lived on this site since the twelfth century. The family still live in a private wing of the house today, and this provides a vital link to Charlecote's past, keeping history alive within this magnificent home.

Above **The bust of Elizabeth I in the Great Hall commemorates the queen's visit to Charlecote in 1572**

Left below **Willement wallpaper in the Library**

Opposite **The west front**

Charlecote and the Lucy Family

The de Lucy or de Luce family originated in Lucé in Normandy, and arrived in England following the Norman Conquest of 1066.

Richard de Luce was the sheriff of the County of Essex, and was excommunicated by Thomas Becket in 1166. In 1189 William de Cherlecote married Cecily de Lucy, and they founded the Lucy family line.

The Tudor mansion

The family's wealth came from owning land and making advantageous marriages. Around 1546 Thomas Lucy married an heiress, Joyce Acton, and in 1551, when he inherited Charlecote, he demolished the original medieval house and built a substantial mansion of brick, which was completed in 1558. Thomas was knighted in 1565 and was honoured by a visit from Queen Elizabeth in 1572. Following his death in 1600, Charlecote was inherited by his son, Sir Thomas Lucy II, then his grandson, also called Thomas. A friend of the poet John Donne, Sir Thomas Lucy III was a scholarly man who loved books.

Completing the formal garden

Colonel George completed the elaborate formal garden begun by his cousin, and undertook major improvements, funded by his second wife, Jane Bohun, who brought valuable property in Spitalfields in London into the family. Colonel Lucy died in 1721, leaving Charlecote to his brother, the Reverend William Lucy, who passed it on to his nephew Thomas, who suffered from epilepsy.

A gentleman of fashion

In 1744 'Bachelor George' Lucy inherited Charlecote from his brother Thomas. He was a gentleman of fashion, a keen traveller and a hypochondriac. He was painted in Rome by Batoni and in Bath by Gainsborough. He engaged 'Capability' Brown to transform the formal gardens into romantic parkland, and in time the estate passed to his cousin, the Reverend John Hammond, who took the name of Lucy.

Upheavals

Successive Lucy heirs were caught up in the political upheavals of the seventeenth century. Spencer Lucy supported King Charles I, and found himself on the losing side; his brother Robert inherited in 1649, owning Charlecote throughout the Commonwealth (1649–53). In 1658 the third brother, Richard, inherited, eventually being granted a royal pardon after Charles II was restored to the throne in 1660. His son Thomas fought in the Anglo-Dutch wars of the 1670s, and began work on a formal water garden in the Dutch style at Charlecote. On his death, as he was childless, the house passed to the descendants of Thomas III's youngest son. Davenport Lucy was killed at the siege of Limerick in 1690, so it was his brother Colonel George Lucy who brought to an end a confusing period in the ownership of the estate.

Opposite far left The tomb of Sir Thomas Lucy I in St Leonard's church

Opposite near left Sir Thomas Lucy III

Above left Richard Lucy

Left Captain Thomas Lucy in 1680

Transformation and decline

In 1823 George Hammond Lucy inherited Charlecote from his father, and promptly married Mary Elizabeth Williams, the daughter of a baronet. Together, they transformed the house in a re-interpretation of the Elizabethan style.

They had eight children, and travelled extensively, and Mary Elizabeth wrote a fascinating account of her life when in her eighties. *Mistress of Charlecote* remains in print and is an invaluable source of information about the house. *(See pp.12–13 for the detailed story of George and Mary Elizabeth.)*

Mary Elizabeth was widowed in 1845, and her eldest son William Fulke Lucy only outlived his father by two years. His brother, Henry Spencer Lucy, was a keen sportsman, but when he and his mother Mary Elizabeth both died in 1890, the house was let for eight years, while Henry's widow Christina and their three daughters lived in her native Scotland. Ada, the eldest girl, was persuaded to marry Henry Ramsay-Fairfax, and they returned to Charlecote when she inherited it. However, the marriage was unhappy; Ada endured 10 pregnancies and was forced to mothball the house, shrouding unused rooms in dust-sheets, and selling off large parts of the estate to pay the bills, while her husband wrote letters to *The Times* bemoaning the plight of the landowner. James Lees-Milne, the National Trust's country house secretary, described Sir Henry as 'pernickety', and, and when he died

in 1944, Charlecote passed to Sir Montgomerie Fairfax-Lucy. A year later, he generously presented it to the National Trust. In 1946, his brother Brian praised 'those uncounted generations of servants who worked so loyally and faithfully for the preservation of this place. Charlecote is as much a memorial to them as to my own ancestors'.

Left Henry Spencer Lucy on the terrace

Opposite above Sir Montgomerie Fairfax-Lucy, who generously gave Charlecote to the National Trust in 1946

Opposite below Alice Fairfax-Lucy

Edmund Fairfax-Lucy is the son of Brian and Alice. He is a painter who trained at the City & Guilds and the Royal Academy Schools. He lives with his family in the south wing, overlooking the Gatehouse, at the heart of the estate, where his ancestors have lived for more than eight centuries.

Returned to splendour

The National Trust accepted the house because of its literary associations, which were perpetuated by Brian's wife Alice, daughter of the novelist John Buchan, who acted as the family's historian and archivist. The 1830s Elizabethan Revival restoration of Charlecote had been seen as a stylistic aberration, but in the 1970s this was re-evaluated. On behalf of the National Trust, John Hardy and Clive Wainwright reinstated the interiors to their early nineteenth-century heyday.

Shakespeare and Charlecote

The legend persists that around 1583, the young William Shakespeare (1564–1616) came from his home town of Stratford-upon-Avon to embark on a poaching expedition in Fulbrook, to the north of Charlecote Park, and was apprehended.

He was brought before the resident magistrate, Sir Thomas Lucy I, who meted out justice in the Great Hall. Poaching by night was a capital offence, but Shakespeare may have pleaded in mitigation that he was rabbit-hunting by day, which carried a lesser sentence. According to the legend, he escaped with a fine and a possible flogging. In retaliation, he wrote a ribald rhyme about the knight and stuck it on the gateway, before heading to London to seek his fame and fortune.

The playwright's revenge

The playwright did not forget his brush with the law, and parodied Sir Thomas Lucy as a querulous, self-serving judge, first in *Henry IV Part II*, and then in *The Merry Wives of Windsor*. The character of Justice Shallow complains to Falstaff 'You have beaten my men, killed my deer, and broken open my lodge,' a clear reference to poaching. Shakespeare also refers to the 'dozen white lucies' in Shallow's coat of arms – a luce is a pike, and for centuries had been the distinctive heraldic motif on the Lucy family's coat of arms.

Shakespeare also pokes fun at Justice Shallow's pride over his 'old coat' of arms; Sir Thomas was known to be proud of his ancestry, evident in the heraldic stained glass he commissioned for the Great Hall, which Shakespeare would have seen while he was being tried. Sir Thomas would boast to friends 'and a very old coat it is too', words Shakespeare put in Justice Shallow's mouth. In *Henry IV Part II*, Falstaff plans to get hold of some of Justice Shallow's money, as surely as the large pike makes a meal of small fish, and refers to him contemptuously as 'the old pike'. Justice Shallow is also portrayed as sitting on the Commission of Array, a post that Sir Thomas held in 1565.

MR. WILLIAM
SHAKESPEARES
COMEDIES,
HISTORIES, and
TRAGEDIES.
Published according to the true Originall Copies.
The second Impression.

LONDON,
Printed by *Tho. Cotes*, for *Robert Allot*, and are to be sold at the signe of the Blacke Beare in Pauls Church-yard. 1 6 3 2.

Opposite Joseph Nash's romantic reconstruction of the poaching incident

Left below The bust of Shakespeare in the Great Hall is based on the playwright's monument in Holy Trinity church, Stratford-upon-Avon

Left above Shakespeare's 1632 Second Folio, from the Library

The legend revived
There is no conclusive evidence about the links between Shakespeare and Charlecote, but the story first appeared in print in 1709 in Nicholas Rowe's brief biography, *Some Account of the Life of Mr William Shakespear (sic)*. The tale was revived in 1769 at the Shakespeare Jubilee, organised by David Garrick. Hanging in the Servants' Corridor there is a fanciful illustration of the poaching incident by Joseph Nash in 1841. It depicts the young Shakespeare caught red-handed by Sir Thomas outside the Gatehouse. The Lucy family were keen to mark the connection with Shakespeare, and George and Mary Elizabeth bought a bust of the playwright for the Great Hall, and some magnificent early volumes of his work for the Library at Charlecote (see pp.26–7).

Mistress of Charlecote: Mary Elizabeth Lucy

Mary Elizabeth Williams grew up at Bodelwyddan Castle in North Wales. She married George Hammond Lucy in 1823 and they travelled to Charlecote, her new home.

Accustomed to every domestic comfort, Mary Elizabeth was horrified by the 'old worn stone floor, its small panes of glass, and old window-frames creaking and rattling with every gust of wind, and so cold!' Fastidious Mary Elizabeth was also shocked to find there were only two earth closets serving the entire household. It was imperative to improve Charlecote, and plumbing was installed, as well as modern plate glass in the main windows.

Charlecote 're-edified'

George Lucy wanted to 're-edify' the house, to remove Georgian additions and return the rooms to how they looked in the 'Golden Age' era of the first Sir Thomas, but incorporating all the technological refinements available to a sophisticated, wealthy family of the 1830s. It was the visiting novelist Sir Walter Scott who inspired George to create a magnificent neo-Elizabethan Great Hall, decorated with family portraits, antlers and heraldic devices. Further improvements included a new service wing, containing a kitchen, scullery and servants' hall, with more bedrooms upstairs. George and Mary Elizabeth also commissioned a new Dining Room and Library, all in a style which recalled Charlecote's heyday.

The Lucys embarked on a spending spree, buying significant Old Master paintings by artists such as Van Dyck, Raphael and Teniers.

George Lucy spent a fortune on the collection of aesthete William Beckford, and they patronised London dealers, buying what they erroneously believed to be 'Elizabethan' artefacts, such as ebony furniture.

Grand Tour tragedy

In 1841–43 the Lucys made a Continental tour in a coach and a carriage, with their children, a tutor, a nurse, a footman, three tin baths and a great deal of luggage. The family visited Paris, Genoa, Rome, Naples and Venice, and spent lavishly on objects for Charlecote. However their 'Grand Tour' was tinged by tragedy; one young son perished as they crossed the Alps. In 1845 George Lucy died, leaving Mary Elizabeth a widow with five surviving children, aged between two and 20. The estate was in serious financial difficulties, but Mary Elizabeth refused to leave Charlecote or to sell any of its holdings. Instead she had St Leonard's Church rebuilt in her husband's memory, and added bay windows to the wings of the east front and balustraded steps down to the river on the west front. She virtually rebuilt the north wing, creating the Drawing Room and Billiard Room.

Memories of eight decades

In old age, Mary Elizabeth wrote her autobiography in five black notebooks with marbled end-papers, bought from a stationers in Warwick. She recorded her memories of eight decades of family life, the vicissitudes and triumphs, and central to her account was her beloved Charlecote, '… that dear old place where sorrow and happiness have been so intertwined'.

Opposite **George Hammond Lucy**

Above **Mary Elizabeth Lucy**

Heraldry and Thomas Willement

George Lucy inherited the family's sense of pride in their ancient lineage and was keen to celebrate it in heraldic designs.

He commissioned a lavishly illuminated pedigree of the family from the College of Arms, tracing the Lucy line back to the time of Edmund Ironside (King Edmund II). He also engaged Thomas Willement (1786–1871) to mastermind the decoration of the principal rooms at Charlecote.

An artist in glass

Willement was fascinated by historic stained glass. Contemporary architects and their clients were increasingly interested in the art and artefacts of the pre-industrial past. Willement's heraldic glass, made using traditional techniques, was popular with his wealthy clients, and he became the armorial painter to George IV, and 'Artist in Stained Glass' to Queen Victoria. He worked with Gothic Revivalist Augustus Pugin, created the stained glass for St George's Chapel at Windsor, and exhibited at the Great Exhibition in London in 1851.

Above **Deer hide decorated with the Lucy family tree**

Above right *The Genealogy of George Lucy* traced his descent back to Edmund Ironside

At Charlecote, Willement repaired the original Tudor glass in the Great Hall, which portrayed the Lucy genealogy up to 1558. He then used the Lucy family pedigree to provide new stained glass windows in the Dining Room and Library. He designed the grained and stencilled plaster ceiling for the Great Hall, and the neo-Elizabethan plaster ceilings in the Library and Dining Room. Willement also designed convincingly sixteenth- and seventeenth-century-looking items which were unknown in the Elizabethan age, such as fitted bookcases, pile carpets and door handles adorned with Tudor roses. In designing the flock wallpaper for the Library, he took as inspiration the fabric of the children's dresses portrayed in the 1619 Lucy family portrait hanging in the Great Hall.

William Beckford and Charlecote

William Beckford (1759–1844) was a playboy, a polymath, a novelist, MP, aesthete and prolific art collector. He built Fonthill Abbey in Wiltshire and Lansdown Tower (Beckford's Tower) in Bath. He used his considerable inherited fortune, derived from slave plantations in Jamaica, to acquire antiques, often bought on his trips around Europe. However, he was forced to sell his beloved home in 1822, and its contents were auctioned over seven weeks during 1823. George Lucy was one of the most avid buyers at the sale, buying 64 lots, and his copy of the sale catalogue is in the Library. George spent £3640 (the equivalent of approximately £155,000 in today's money), and he even outbid King George IV to acquire a magnificent *pietra dura* table.

Above left **Heraldic stained glass by Willement**

Above right **Willement wallpaper in the Dining Room**

Left **Fonthill vase**

Exploring Charlecote
The Gatehouse

The Gatehouse is a Renaissance gem, constructed in the tradition of fortified buildings of the Middle Ages, a more dangerous era, when important houses feared attack.

The Charlecote Gatehouse was erected by Sir Thomas Lucy I in 1565, a time of peace, and bears the coat of arms of his grandson, Sir Thomas Lucy III. It was intended as a status symbol, to impress visitors approaching the house. Built of a mellow red-brick with grey stone balustrading, each of the two octagonal towers is capped with an ogee-shaped lead cupola. The underside of the central arch has heavy stone vaulting and ceiling bosses in the Gothic style, but the shell-headed alcoves set into the walls are more classically-inspired Jacobean. On either side of the arch are the former gate-keepers' rooms (one of which now provides you with an introductory tour.)

At first-floor level is a large room where the family would occasionally retire after dinner for a final course of sweet 'banquet' delicacies. This is now the Lucy family museum, housing a

diverse collection of nineteenth-century sporting items. Cricket, tennis, polo, fishing, croquet, boxing and archery are represented here, along with details of hunting fixtures, game books and examples of taxidermy.

The banqueting room is dominated by a colossal refectory table which belonged to Sir Thomas Lucy III. Despite its size and weight, it has been moved several times between the Great Hall and the Servants' Hall, before being installed in the Gatehouse. The table was hewn from a single massive oak tree trunk. At 19 feet (approx 6 metres) in length, it is one of the largest surviving Jacobean tables in England. Visitors can also hear the thump, crash and whirr of the venerable Gatehouse clock, as it gears up to chime. It dates from 1824.

Above The Gatehouse

Left The Banqueting Room

The Green Court and Forecourt

The Green Court is the rectangular space which runs from the Gatehouse to the façade of the manor house.

It is bounded by a brick wall screening the stable buildings and brew-house to the south, and a corresponding nineteenth-century wall with a stone parapet of elongated rosettes copied from the gatehouse balustrade along the north. The gravel path along the north–south axis takes visitors through pairs of much-repaired eighteenth-century wrought-iron gates.

In the Victorian era, the Forecourt close to the entrance porch was laid out as an Elizabethan *parterre,* with gravel walks and low box hedges enclosing geometrically arranged flower-beds. This layout was simplified in the 1950s for ease of maintenance, but a new garden designed by Sir Edmund Fairfax-Lucy was laid out in 2000. It is based on the mathematical relationships he discovered between the house, gatehouse and forecourt enclosure.

Right Lead statue of a shepherdess by Edward Hurst

The entrance front

Although it looks like the quintessential Elizabethan country house, in fact Charlecote has been much enlarged and altered by successive generations of the same family, since its sixteenth-century origins.

Building work started in 1551, when Thomas Lucy I inherited the property and used his heiress wife's money to remove the old house and replace it with one of the first great houses of the Elizabethan era. The new Charlecote was in plan a half-H, facing east–west, and the manor house was probably completed by 1558, the date found on the earliest of the heraldic stained glass in the Great Hall, which proclaims Thomas Lucy's pride in his ancient lineage.

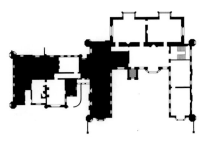

A red-brick patchwork

The sixteenth-century house was built of warm red brick, made at Bishops Hampton (now Hampton Lucy), and ornamented with Warwickshire stone. It had stair turrets at the corners, housing spiral staircases. However, the Elizabethan-style chimneys and the bay windows to be seen today actually date from the early nineteenth century. The Lucy family also rebuilt much of this frontage, which is apparent from the 'patchwork' of different brickwork. In fact, like many venerable mansions, Charlecote grew and changed over many centuries, reflecting the waxing and waning fortunes of its many owners.

The main façade has two protruding wings flanking an impressive two-storeyed entrance porch. In the centre, behind the large bay window, is the Great Hall. The north wing to the right comprises a ground floor containing the mid-Victorian Billiard Room and Drawing Room, with a suite of bedrooms above. The south wing to the left is the home of the Fairfax-Lucy family and is not accessible to visitors.

The entrance porch

The most impressive sixteenth-century feature is the two-storeyed entrance porch, off-centre in the manner of medieval examples, but resolutely Renaissance in style, with pillars of the composite order. It was built about 1565, and was later emblazoned with Queen Elizabeth's coat of arms, following her visit in 1572. Famed for her peripatetic 'progresses' around her realm, and notorious for bringing with her an enormous entourage, the queen was visiting *en route* from nearby Kenilworth, the home of her favourite, Robert Dudley. It was Dudley who had knighted the first Sir Thomas Lucy in the Great Hall at Charlecote in 1565, on behalf of the Queen. The visit of the great monarch seven years later conferred a great deal of prestige on the family, and the Elizabethan heritage was much-revisited by later owners of Charlecote.

Opposite The entrance front

Left The porch

The Great Hall

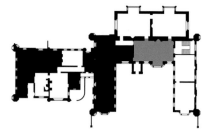

In the sixteenth and seventeenth centuries, this room acted as the principal chamber in which guests were greeted and entertained.

Although this part of the house was completed in 1558, many of its present-day features were created in the 1830s by George and Mary Elizabeth Lucy, who wanted to make improvements to the venerable property. They employed Thomas Willement (see p.14) to make over the dilapidated Great Hall in Elizabethan Revival style, in honour of Charlecote's most illustrious visitor. The minstrels' gallery and the panelling were removed, and the organ was donated to Hampton Lucy Church. A new flattened barrel-vault ceiling was created in plaster and painted to look like timber. The brick walls were plastered and painted in imitation of stonework. The impressive chimneypiece appears to be Elizabethan, but is also a nineteenth-century interpretation. The red and white marble floor was bought by the Lucys in Venice while on the Grand Tour and laid in 1844. The ancient flagstones it replaced were re-laid in the service wing.

Furniture

Much of the grand furniture in this room was bought by George and Mary Elizabeth Lucy. The centrepiece is the magnificent sixteenth-century table top made of *pietra dura* (literally, 'hard stone'), a technique using inlaid coloured marble and semi-precious stones, which originated in Italy. It is believed that this was removed from the Borghese Palace in Rome during Napoleon's Italian campaign in 1796, and taken to Paris, where it was bought by the connoisseur William Beckford. He commissioned the Gothic-style oak frame for it, but was forced to sell it in 1823. George Lucy bought it in the famous Fonthill Abbey sale of 1823 for 1,800 guineas, approximately £80,000 in today's money, outbidding even King George IV to acquire it. The table top alone weighs 2290 lbs (1038 kilos) and measures 9 feet x 4 feet 6 inches (275 x 135.5 cms). The four small Gothic tables also came from the Fonthill sale, and two further copies were made for the Lucys. The 'antique' sideboard was purchased for the Dining Room in 1837, but was moved into the Great Hall in 1858.

Stained glass

When the house was first built in 1558, the upper panes of the bay window of the Great Hall were filled with heraldic stained glass, tracing the Lucy lineage back to medieval times. The designs were created by Nicholas Eyffeler, who was born in Germany and was commissioned by the first Sir Thomas Lucy. Nearly three centuries later, Willement repaired and releaded the original glass, and continued the genealogical sequence around the other windows of the room, adding eight further panels.

Opposite The Great Hall

Below The *pietra dura* table

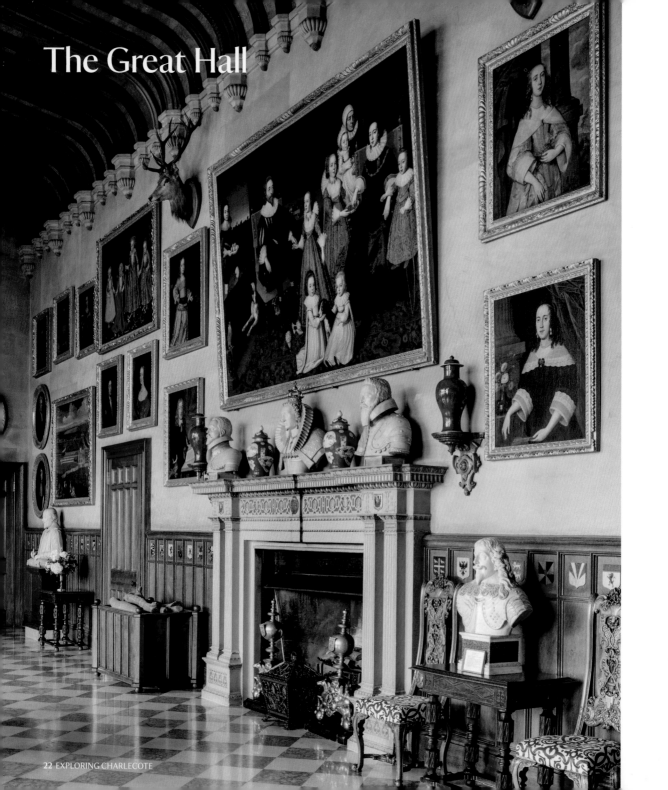

The Great Hall

The Lucys celebrated their forebears in the numerous family portraits gathered in the Great Hall.

Paintings

Above the fireplace is a group portrait of *Sir Thomas Lucy III and his Family*, of around 1625. Sir Thomas and his wife Alice are portrayed taking dessert with seven of their thirteen children; the hawk and book on the side table show Sir Thomas's love of hunting and reading. In this busy household, the children were instructed to be silent in the presence of elders, courteous to visitors, and banned from using their catapults indoors. Over the door to the Dining Room is an earlier portrait of 1619, depicting four of Thomas and Alice's children, Robert (aged 2), one-year-old Richard, seated in the chair. It was Richard Lucy (c.1619–77), who inherited Charlecote in 1658, and managed to preserve the property despite the political turmoil of the Commonwealth and Restoration. In a nearby mahogany glass-topped case is a 'Writ of Sumons', a handwritten letter from Oliver Cromwell to Richard Lucy, commanding him to attend the 'Barebones' Parliament as MP for the County of Warwick in 1653, '… And hereof you are not to fail.'

The *View of Charlecote Park*, painted in the late seventeenth century, portrays a more stable phase in the family's history. It depicts the Elizabethan west façade, before it was extended towards the river in the early 1830s, and the Dutch-style garden that was swept away in 1760. It is therefore an important record of the development of the property. In the foreground are a group of picnickers, including Colonel George Lucy (died 1721) and his first wife, Mary, who created the formal garden.

On either side of the doors to the stairs are oval portraits of George Hammond Lucy and his wife Mary Elizabeth, whose vision created the Great Hall.

Sculpture

Matching busts of George Hammond and Mary Elizabeth sculpted by William Behnes, in Carrara marble, dating from 1830, flank the bay window. At the centre is the tall alabaster vase with four carved doves on the brim, by Pisani, which they bought in Florence in 1841. The design was based on a classical mosaic in Hadrian's Villa near Rome. The Lucys were particularly fond of sculpture, and they commemorated the two most famous visitors to Charlecote in this medium. The bust of Queen Elizabeth in the centre of the mantelpiece was copied from Maximilian Colt's tomb effigy of the monarch in Westminster Abbey (1605–7), with a crown added. To the left of the Dining Room door is a bust of William Shakespeare, poacher turned playwright.

Above The alabaster vase with four carved doves

Opposite Family portraits fill the Great Hall

Below Group portrait of Sir Thomas Lucy III and his family

The Dining Room

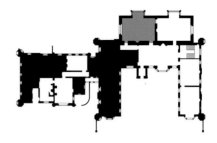

Between 1833 and 1837, the Lucys added a major extension to the west front of Charlecote.

They wanted a magnificent dining room where they could entertain, with large windows providing extensive views over the River Avon, the deer-park and the rolling countryside. During dinner one night, Mary Elizabeth ordered the candles extinguished, and the family thrilled as a spectacular thunderstorm lit up the landscape.

Willement's Elizabethan

As in the Great Hall, Thomas Willement drew on historical examples to design the Dining Room in an Elizabethan Revival style. He created the rich wallpaper of crimson and blue flock on a gold ground, which cost 5 shillings a yard, totalling £71 17s 6d. The smaller Axminster carpet under the mahogany dining table bears heraldic motifs of the Lucy family, and was also designed by Willement. The dining chairs by the same designer were purchased in 1837 for £158 13s 6d.

He filled the upper compartments of the windows with coloured armorial glass, celebrating the Lucy family's genealogy.

The richly ornamented plaster ceiling is based on that of the King James Drawing Room at Hatfield House in Hertfordshire. Each pendant was cast in plaster, with a bolt protruding from the top, which was then threaded into a nut inserted into the ceiling joists.

The Charlecote Buffet

Over the chimneypiece is a large painting by the Flemish artist Frans Snyders (1579–1657), entitled *Spoils of the Game Larder*. On a similar theme, the colossal Charlecote Buffet dominates one side of the room. The carvings depict the diverse fruits of nature from the land and the sea, together with figures of a fisherman and a hunter. It was carved by local craftsman, J.M. Willcox of Warwick and his apprentices, and was initially offered to Queen Victoria, who was visiting Warwickshire, but she declined it. Willcox also provided the fine oak panelling around the

Dining Room. Made of oak, the sideboard took five years to complete. The dogs' heads drawer handles depicted Willcox's own pets. To enhance the glow of the silver, the buffet was fitted with Argand oil lamps. It was bought by Mary Elizabeth Lucy in 1858 as a gift for her eldest surviving son Henry Spencer, for the huge sum of £1,600, and was used to display silver plate.

Silver

Important silver is on show in this room; the Princes' Centrepiece was given by Prince Eddy, Duke of Clarence and eldest grandson of Queen Victoria, and his brother Prince George (later King George V) to Henry Fairfax in 1879, after they had completed their naval training at Dartmouth under him. The original is on show at Sandringham House. The ornate silver centrepiece was commissioned in 1842 as a gift to Thomas Williamson in recognition of his work as a revenue commissioner in Bombay. The silver dessert knives and forks on the table were made by consummate silversmith Paul Storr in 1813, while the Adam-style candelabra date from 1790–1.

Opposite The Dining Room

Above left The Elizabethan Revival plasterwork ceiling

Left The Charlecote Buffet

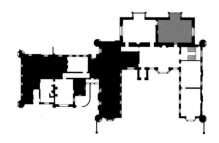

The Library

Charlecote has one of the National Trust's finest country house libraries, containing nearly 3,500 volumes.

'Live to learn, learn to live'

The Library was built between 1833 and 1837 by George Lucy and his wife Mary Elizabeth; their motto, 'Live to learn, learn to live' and their initials are carved on the magnificent fireplace, below the portrait of Queen Elizabeth I.

Thomas Willement designed the neo-Elizabethan bookcases, the carved woodwork, and the carpet with its heraldic motifs, including the Lucy pike. Willement's stained glass windows record the family's marriages. He designed the brown flock and gold leaf wallpaper and the matching chintz covers on the seat furniture (now covered with reproductions from about 1954). Warwick woodcarver Willcox, who created the vast buffet in the Dining Room, also executed the carved decorations on the Library bookcases.

In 1837 the Lucys acquired a pair of cabinets and a suite of ebony seat furniture inlaid with ivory, believing they had been a present to Queen Elizabeth from the Earl of Leicester, but they were made in Vizagapatam in India around 1700. The seat cushions were embroidered by Mary Elizabeth. The *pietra dura* table top in the bay window was purchased in London in 1824 for 500 guineas, while the casket in the same material on the octagonal table was bought by the Lucys during their Grand Tour.

George also acquired a number of antique Greek vases, dating from between the 6th and 4th centuries BC, though one is a Victorian replica. Originally found in the ruins of Pompeii or Herculaneum, antique vases were highly prized by connoisseurs for their associations with classical learning. Because of their fragility, it is rare to find examples still in country house libraries.

The pair of celestial and terrestrial (the heavens and the earth) globes, mounted on Chippendale-style mahogany stands, was made by W. & T.M. Bardin *c*.1799.

Rare books

The Library contains some notable rarities, including an exquisite illuminated late fourteenth-century *Book of Hours,* and an early sixteenth-century manuscript copy of Machiavelli's *The Prince.* This is one of the most important surviving copies of the definitive Renaissance work on politics and power.

Above An ancient Greek black-figure vase, *c*.500 BC

Opposite The Library

Left Erasmus presented Henry VIII with this copy of his *Institutio Principis Christiani*, which was illuminated by Holbein

In 1828, George Lucy was given the Second Folio of Shakespeare, a compilation of his 'Comedies, Histories and Tragedies', of 1632, one of the Library's great treasures. A decade later he bought a second quarto copy of *The Merry Wives of Windsor*, by William Shakespeare, published in 1619. Other highlights include Abraham Ortelius's *Theatrum Orbis Terrarum* of 1570, one of earliest atlases ever published, and the unique

presentation copy of *Institutio Principis Christiani* by Desiderius Erasmus, which was given to Henry VIII by the author in 1516.

'There were some fine old books… How odd if a folio of Shakespeare should be found amongst them…'

Sir Walter Scott, following his visit to Charlecote, 1828

The Billiard Room

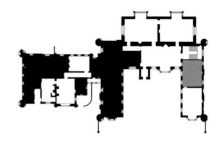

Billiard rooms were the favoured haunt of many Victorian gentlemen anxious for exclusively masculine company, the opportunity to smoke, gossip and play the fashionable game.

A gentleman of fashion

The accomplished 'swagger' portrait of 'Bachelor George' Lucy (1714–86) dominates the Billiard Room. It was painted in Rome in 1758 and cost 40 guineas. George was on the Grand Tour but letters reveal his favourite clothes had been

chimneypiece complete with Lucy heraldry, which was purchased in Florence in 1841.

The mahogany billiard table (not the original) dates from the mid-1850s and, as traditional, has a slate bed. Consequently it is very heavy; billiard rooms were nearly always installed on the ground floor for structural reasons. The accompanying furniture is notably masculine in style, though there are some small pieces of lacquer and a pair of grey eighteenth-century Japanese ceramic vases, all of which came from the Fonthill sale. An early nineteenth-century pair of Chinese pagodas carved from soapstone are adorned with metal bells.

Portraits

Numerous family portraits are shown in this room, including one of Henry Spencer Lucy (1830–90), eldest surviving son of George and Mary Elizabeth. A dedicated sportsman, Henry sold a number of Charlecote's best paintings, smuggling them out of the house while his mother was asleep. Henry's daughter, Ada (1866–1943), who inherited Charlecote in 1890, is portrayed with her eldest son William, who died while a pupil at Eton in 1910. Ada's husband Henry Fairfax (1870–1944) helped shoulder the daunting financial burden of running the estate. There is also an attractive portrait by William Rothenstein of Alice Fairfax-Lucy, the mother of the present baronet. She was the daughter of John Buchan, famed for writing *The Thirty-Nine Steps*. Alice published *Charlecote and the Lucys* in 1958, and edited *Mistress of Charlecote* by Mary Elizabeth Lucy, which was published in 1983.

Opposite **The Billiard Room**

Above left 'Bachelor George' Lucy was painted in Rome by Pompeo Batoni

Above **The Chinese pagodas were carved from soapstone**

taken by Moorish pirates, so he may be wearing borrowed or replacement finery in this painting. As a gentleman of fashion, he was keen to engage the services of the famous Italian artist Pompeo Batoni, but the experience was not entirely a happy one. He commented, 'These painters are great men, and must be flattered, for 'tis the custom here, not to think themselves obliged to you for employing them, but that they oblige you by being employed.'

Bachelor retreat

Mary Elizabeth had a former dining room in the north wing remodelled in the 1850s to provide her male guests with a 'bachelor retreat' – today's Billiard Room. The ladies would retire to the 'Withdrawing Room' next door. Little of the original decorative scheme remains on the walls here, but the 1856 shallow-ribbed ceiling in the 'Jacobean' style survives, as does the marble

The Drawing Room

It is believed by some that Queen Elizabeth I stayed in this room during her visit in 1572. In the 1850s, it was transformed into an elegant 'withdrawing room', where ladies conversed or played music after dinner.

Mary Elizabeth's Erard harp graces the room; this was the third instrument she owned, and it dates from 1844. She was an accomplished musician, and was tutored by Queen Victoria's harpist, John Thomas, a frequent visitor and valued family friend.

'Mr Thomas came to Charlecote soon after our return…Everyone was in raptures with his playing. Lady Louisa Percy said she had never liked the harp till she heard Mr Thomas who had simply enchanted her!'

Mistress of Charlecote

Above right **Mary Elizabeth's Erard harp**

Below left **The neo-Jacobean ceiling**

Below right **The *pietra dura* cabinet**

Opposite **The Drawing Room**

The amber-coloured silk wall-hangings were handwoven in 1984, identical replacements for the originals. A mid-Victorian 'Jacobean' plaster ceiling recalls the earlier historic heyday of Charlecote, an effect reinforced by the portraits of Richard III, Henry VIII and Mary Tudor.

Portraits

The portrait of 'Bachelor George' Lucy (1714–86) was painted in Bath by Thomas Gainsborough in 1760, and cost eight guineas, plus three guineas for the frame. A later portrait is that of Alice Fairfax-Lucy by John Morley, standing by the 1722 Nicholas Paris gates in the grounds.

Furniture from Fonthill

The room contains some of the best furniture and oriental ceramics that the Lucys acquired from the Fonthill Abbey sale. The large cabinet contains *pietra dura* panels made in Florence c.1620, while the smaller cabinet was purchased in Florence; both are supported by matching stands commissioned by William Beckford.

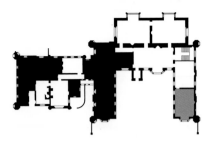

There is a *pietra dura* casket which is believed to have come from the Pitti Palace in Florence. The pair of Boulle cabinets are masterpieces of the skilful technique, which combines brass and tortoiseshell in intricate patterns, and their ebony stands bear an armorial device used by Beckford.

The seventeenth-century East India settee was acquired in London in 1827, and the other chairs were bought soon after. Ebony seat furniture was highly fashionable in this era, the lasting legacy of Horace Walpole, who had used it at his 'Gothick' home, Strawberry Hill, in the belief that it was Tudor. The Indian carved teak *tête-à-tête* settee dates from the mid-nineteenth century, and was designed for courting couples.

Spoils of war

The eighteenth-century ceremonial dress sword was captured at the Relief of Lucknow in September 1857. It is made of silver inlaid with garnets and turquoises, and was brought to Charlecote by Captain Powllet Lane, who had fought in the Indian Mutiny. He married Carrie, one of the daughters of George and Mary Elizabeth.

Please ascend the steep turret staircase in the corner to the first floor, or ask a room steward for the easier route if required.

The Ebony Bedroom

With picturesque views across the Green Court to the Gatehouse, this family bedroom dates from the sixteenth century, and may have been used by 'Bachelor George' in the eighteenth century. Here it is presented as it was described in the comprehensive 1891 inventory, and by reference to detailed paint analysis.

The dominant feature is the impressive ebony bed made for William Beckford from a seventeenth-century Indian settee. Known as the Lancaster State Bed while it was at Fonthill Abbey, it was purchased by George Hammond Lucy in 1837 from the auctioneer Edward English of Bath. It came complete with hangings, two feather mattresses, and a silk quilt, and cost £140 5s 6d.

Above The Ebony Bedroom

The cornice was added to match the classical door surrounds of the bedroom. The ebonised wash-stands, tables and bed-steps (which conceal a chamber-pot) were all made in the 1830s to match the bed, and the writing set and brass candlesticks also date from the same period.

The large-scale trellis-patterned wallpaper replicates a pattern formerly used in the house, while the Brussels-weave carpet is a copy of a mid-nineteenth-century pattern also at Charlecote.

The panel of Wliiams family miniatures is believed to be by Thomas Hargreaves (1774–1847). He was commissioned by Mary Elizabeth to paint her nurse, parents and four sisters shortly before her marriage to George. Mary Elizabeth wanted the paintings as mementoes of her former life at Bodelwyddan, before she became mistress of Charlecote, and she paid 10 guineas for each.

The Sultan and the Sahib

Two other important and unique miniature portraits in this room echo the Indian theme. One depicts Tipu Sultan (1749–99), the phenomenally wealthy and powerful Sultan of Mysore, who was killed during the storming of Seringapatam by the forces of the British East India Company and their allies. One column was led by Arthur Wellesley, who later became the Duke of Wellington. Tipu Sultan died in the battle, and was described in death by an eyewitness Benjamin Sydenham as having:

'…large full eyes, with small arched eyebrows and very small whiskers. His appearance denoted him to be above the common stamp.'

The Victoria & Albert Museum has a famous wooden automaton known as 'Tipu's Tiger', which belonged to the sultan, a trophy from Seringapatam. The second painting is said to portray Nana Sahib, the head of the Sepoys (Indian servicemen), who led the rebellion in Cawnpore (now Kanpur) during the 1857 uprising against British rule.

Above **Tipu Sultan**

Below **The miniatures are mainly of Mary Elizabeth's Welsh relations and servants**

The Visitors' Corridor and bedrooms

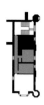

During the Victorian era, both wings of the house contained family bedrooms, but the South Wing is now the Lucy family's private residence.

For more than 50 years, this section of Charlecote was used for NT staff accommodation and was closed to the public, but in 2000 the corridor and adjacent suite of rooms were opened up to visitors. Following extensive research by the National Trust, the decorative graining was repaired, and the walls repainted in colours used in the early Victorian era. The Brussels weave carpet was remade to replicate the design used on the main staircase. The rooms' contents were reinstated in keeping with the details listed in the 1891 inventory.

Until the early twentieth century, these rooms were allocated to male visitors, particularly bachelors.

Opposite The Visitors' Corridor

Below The Ebony Dressing Room

The Ebony Dressing Room
This is arranged as for use by a gentleman guest about to wash and change before dinner. On the

bed are his evening clothes, carefully laid out by a valet or manservant. Washing facilities include a wash-stand, hip-bath, pot cupboard and footbath. As this part of the house had no integral plumbing, large jugs of hot water for baths and washing would be carried up the spiral stairs in the corner turret by servants, and they would also discreetly remove chamber pots and slops.

The Orange Bedroom
Next door is another guest room, the Orange Bedroom, which is open to visitors on restricted days. The wallpaper design of bold strapwork pattern has been reproduced from one of Thomas Willement's designs which survive elsewhere in the house, but the carpet and curtains are original and date from the 1850s. The furniture is shrouded in white cotton sheets, showing how the room would have been while the family were away in London, or holidaying on the Continent. In the nineteenth century, country house furniture and fittings were routinely protected in this way from dust and daylight. A team of housemaids under the control of the housekeeper would 'shut up' rooms which were not in use. Nowadays National Trust staff and volunteers often employ similar methods to conserve fragile interiors.

The Holiday Flat
Above this floor are the attics, which were occupied in the heyday of the house by unmarried female resident servants. These rooms have been converted for modern use and are now rented out as a three-bedroomed holiday flat.

The Staircase Hall

The impressive oak staircase in three flights was commissioned as part of the major interior alterations made between 1717 and 1723 by Colonel George Lucy.

The new staircase was installed by Francis Smith of Warwick (1672–1736), and Joel Lobb, a carver from Warwick, was paid £15 for supplying carvings and decorative mouldings for the staircase. Each tread has three twisted balusters and tread ends. The panelling is from a later date, probably installed in the nineteenth century. Combining domestic practicality with aesthetics, there is a large linen cupboard on the top landing, concealed by the panelling, though the keyhole is visible. It is disguised by the painting attributed to Henri-Pierre Danloux, which depicts Robert Ramsay of Camno and Arthurstown.

Lighting

Illuminating the central well is a large brass lantern with six glass panels. Electricity was first introduced to Charlecote in 1922, and this lantern was converted to run on electricity in 1930.

Portraits and tapestries

The staircase is hung with paintings; of particular note is a portrait by Sir Henry Raeburn, of Thomas Williamson-Ramsay. Two early eighteenth-century Flemish tapestries from the 'Art of War' series depict scenes from the Duke of Marlborough's campaigns in Europe, reflecting Colonel George Lucy's military career.

Furniture

The furniture includes a twentieth-century copy of a Dutch high-backed chair in pearwood, in the style of Daniel Marot, c.1710. A set of six Louis XIV-style chairs were purchased by the Lucys from Samuel Isaacs in London in 1837. The six matching chairs now on show in various rooms at Charlecote are high quality replicas, which were commissioned by Sir Henry Fairfax-Lucy in 1924, before he sold the originals to an American museum for £6000.

The magnificent Dutch cabinet at the foot of the stairs was purchased by the Lucys in 1837 for £50. It was probably made around 1690, by Jan van Mekeren (1658–1733) of Amsterdam, the most renowned cabinet maker of his time. Marquetry uses rich and subtly coloured woods, including sycamore and laburnum, and this design draws on the still-life paintings for which contemporary Netherlands painters were so much in demand.

Opposite The Staircase Hall

Above The van Mekeren cabinet

Return through the Great Hall and exit by the front door, following the signs to the right towards the Service Wing.

The Service Wing and Outbuildings

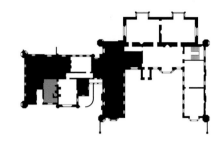

George Lucy had a new service wing built on the site of the kitchen garden in 1829, as Charlecote's many servants needed accommodation, and the old Elizabethan kitchen was both inadequate and outdated. The location of the Georgian wing ensured its distinctive sounds and smells would be remote from the rest of the house.

The ground floor comprised a wide entrance corridor for staff and supplies, with a larder on the left. There was a large kitchen with an adjacent scullery, a still-room, a housekeeper's room and servants' hall. In addition, there were rooms for the butler, footmen and valets, fuel stores and a boot and brushing room. In this part of the house, food was prepared, the family's clothes were maintained, candles and lamps were prepared daily to light the interiors, and the assorted staff worked and had their meals. On the first floor level were the nurseries occupied by the Lucy children and their nannies, as well as extra family bedrooms, all heated by the chimney flue from the kitchen chimney.

The Scullery

The walls were painted powder-blue, as this was thought to be a colour which deterred house-flies.

All fruit and vegetables for use in the kitchen were initially washed and prepared here, using well-water from the pump beside the window before piped water was introduced in the late nineteenth century. Bread was also made here, using the contents of the large flour bin, then baked in the wood-burning oven. The loaves for the household were carefully removed using the paddle-shaped wooden 'peel', and set aside to cool, and cakes, buns and puddings were cooked in the bread oven as the temperature dropped. The oven still works today, and NT volunteers often cook bakery goods in it. This bread oven was succeeded by the New Gold Medal Eagle Range of about 1900, a coal-fired model with two ovens and hot plates, which was much more controllable.

Left The coal-fired Eagle Range in the Scullery

Opposite above The Scullery

Opposite below The ice-box

Charlecote staff in 1851

There were 14 'indoor' staff employed at Charlecote in 1851, according to that year's census, and there was a strict hierarchy. The men were managed by John Foster the butler, aged 54, while Jane Hughes the housekeeper, aged 52, ran the female servants. The servants' quarters remained in use until the 1930s, and although technological innovations were periodically introduced, Charlecote has one of the best surviving Victorian kitchens in Britain.

An early refrigerator

The insulated wooden chest in the corner is an ice-box, an early type of refrigerator. Ice was collected from rivers and ponds in winter and stored in a subterranean ice-house on the estate. Chunks were put in the ice-box as required to chill the iced deserts encased in metal moulds or 'bombes'. Such delicacies were status symbols, and much in demand at country house parties in the era before mechanical refrigeration.

1. The Kitchen

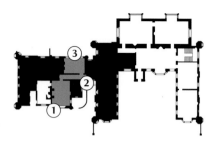

The high ceiling and pitched roof helped disperse the considerable heat generated by cooking.

Large windows which were easy to open also helped control the temperature in this intense working environment. Though modern by Victorian standards, the kitchen floor is Tudor; the worn flagstones which once graced the Great Hall were economically re-used here when that chamber was refurbished in the 1840s.

One of the original roasting spits survives in the smaller, right-hand recess. Large carcases of meat would be cooked in front of the fire, the spit gently rotating mechanically as the heat rose and activated large metal fans fitted in the chimney flue. The 'baffle', a large metal-lined warming cupboard on wheels, both reflected and deflected the fire's radiant heat, augmenting the cooking process of the meat but protecting the cook and staff from extreme temperatures. The left-hand recess contains the 'Prize Kitchener', dating from the 1860s, with its double roasting oven, two single ovens, and hot plates. Next to it is the 'Bon-fire' boiler of about 1928, which supplied hot water to a closed tank which served the kitchen, scullery and nurseries upstairs. The copper *batterie de cuisine* includes a huge *bain marie*, which holds seven smaller saucepans, in which the cook would supervise the making of numerous sauces to accompany the meals.

The central work table was scrubbed every day with eggshells, and was lit from above by a large oil lamp, and it was from here that the cook directed operations, supervising the kitchen maids. Tureens and dishes of food ready to eat were placed on trays on the serving hatch counter, and carried along the corridor, to the family's breakfast or dining table.

2. The Service Corridor

With its venerable, worn flagstones, this corridor runs like a busy thoroughfare through this utilitarian part of Charlecote.

High on the wall are the 24 interior bells, each labelled so that servants could see which room required their services. Every bell has a distinctive tone, which veteran servants could identify by sound, while newcomers relied on seeing which bell was still vibrating. At the far end of the corridor is the substantial oak door leading into the main part of the house. Once through the door, servants considered themselves to be 'on stage', and acted accordingly.

3. The Servants' Hall

This is a large room where the domestic staff ate their meals, received their orders and waited to be 'summoned by bells'.

Any leisure time might also be spent here, reading, sewing or writing letters. The room is now Charlecote's shop. The adjacent housekeeper's parlour and butler's pantry were smaller rooms, but their occupants' higher status brought relative privacy.

Below left The bell-board

Below centre The giant pestle and mortar in the Kitchen

Below right The Kitchen table

The Laundry

The Laundry has medieval stone foundations and was possibly once the site of a small manor house.

The building originally functioned as the bakehouse, and the old bread oven continued to be used by the servants in the nineteenth century, when the family were away. It subsequently became the household's two-storey laundry; downstairs was the 'wet laundry', where the laundress would supervise hand-washing the majority of household's linen. On the floor above (no longer accessible) was the 'dry laundry', where clothes and bed-linens were hung to dry and air before ironing.

A washerwoman's work

Being a washerwoman was a physically demanding job. Fires were lit underneath the coppers and the washing was boiled in water with grated hard soap and lye. The wet clothes were agitated with a wooden 'dolly' to help shift the dirt. By the 1850s there was a resilient fabric newly available, American cotton, which was harder-wearing and easier to wash, and the invention of the mangle made it easier to wring water out of sodden textiles. Nevertheless, it was hard work and poorly rewarded; in 1851, Charlecote's laundress Mary Eboral was 28 years old and earned a meagre £14 per year, though she 'lived in', so did not pay for her rent or board.

The Brew-house

The Brew-house adjoins the Laundry and is a rare survival.

Before the advent of safe mains water in the late nineteenth century, and while tea remained prohibitively expensive, most British households of any size brewed their own beer for home consumption. The beer-making process used boiled water, effectively killing water-born bacteria. An adult man could easily consume 6 or 8 pints of home-brewed beer a day, and it was the main beverage for most classes and both sexes. Beer wasn't always highly alcoholic, as it could be made to different strengths. Country house beers were either 'strong beer' made from the first mash, or weaker 'small beer', made from the second and third mashes of the reused malt. Small beer was drunk by the servants, women and children.

At Charlecote, estate-grown barley was converted into malt in the malt-house in the village, then ground and carted to the brew-house, where the machinery and equipment used in the brewing process can still be seen.

Opposite **The Laundry**
Right **The Brew-house**

Beer was usually made in between October and March, and full barrels were stored in the cellars underneath the house. Family celebrations were also marked by special brews. 400 gallons of a notably strong beer were made for the wedding of Emily Lucy in October 1847:

'… every cottage on the estate was regaled with beef, plum pudding and good ale in the new loft over the stables… everything went well and dancing was kept up with great spirit till four o'clock in the morning…'

Mistress of Charlecote

The Stableyard and surroundings

In the nineteenth century, there were many more outbuildings in active use, as the Charlecote estate was largely self-sufficient, like a small village.

There were game rooms and larders, dog kennels and an ice-house, and the woodyard adjacent to the stableyard was the focal point of workers employed on maintaining the estate, managing the timber, and animal husbandry. Many of the employees lived with their families in cottages on site. It was very much a community, home and workplace to many people.

The Stable-block

Charlecote was reliant on horsepower well into the twentieth century. The Tudor stable-block has Victorian additions; it is an attractive two-storeyed brick-built structure, and in its heyday would have been a hive of activity. Accommodation for the grooms was provided on the first floor, and a large loft was used for social events for the estate workers. The horses, the various vehicles they pulled and the kit and equipment that was needed to manage them were all housed on the ground floor.

Above **The equipment for maintaining and adapting the tack is laid out on the table**

Opposite **The Tack Room**

War horses

There is always a strong bond between those who work with horses and their charges. At the outbreak of World War I, all over Britain horses were requisitioned by the army, to be sent to the battlefields as mounts for cavalry officers or to pull gun-carriages and wagons. Francis Keeble, the Fairfax-Lucys' coachman, volunteered as a soldier, and was sent to France. One evening, he was walking along a tethered line of army horses, when one of them neighed frantically at him. He had been recognised by one of his former coach horses, fondly remembered from happier days at Charlecote.

The Tack Room

The Tack Room was the Head Groom's office, as it was here that he handed out his orders for the day. It was used to keep the household's saddlery and other riding equipment, to maintain and clean it. The fireplace was in use year-round, to eradicate damp and mould which can damage leather and metal. The upper gallery, reached by ladder, provided extra storage space. The variety of equine equipment on show here is remarkable, from side-saddles for ladies, to double seats for small children, horse collars, bits, snaffles, and hoof oil. The leather overshoes displayed on the table were used to muffle the horses' feet when they were drawing a funeral bier. There is also a monogrammed horse-blanket hanging from a rack. The name plates of long-gone horses, such as 'Limelight', survive here and in the neighbouring stables, now a second-hand bookshop.

The Carriages

The Coach-house and Carriage-houses contain Charlecote's unique collection of Victorian horse-drawn vehicles, which was generously given to the National Trust by Sir Edmund Fairfax-Lucy.

The Coach-house

It contains a magnificent, high-sprung travelling coach, c.1845, similar to the one in which George, Mary Elizabeth, their children and their servants travelled throughout Europe in 1841–43. The smaller Victoria coach is of later design, and was used for local visits to neighbours. The Prince of Wales, the future Edward VII, bought a carriage like this for his mother, Queen Victoria, when visiting Paris in 1869, hence the name.

The funeral bier dates from the 1840s, and was used to transport coffins to St Leonard's Church for burial services. It was on this bier, drawn by her favourite pony, that Mary Elizabeth Lucy made her final journey in 1890.

The Stable Carriage-house

The Breaking Cart was used by grooms to train young horses to pull a carriage or coach. The Whitechapel Cart, of about 1870, was favoured by sporting gentlemen for their guns and dogs, as it has high visibility for narrow country lanes and good undercarriage clearance over rough ground. The Lucy ladies often drove themselves and up to three passengers in the Battlesden Car, which was pulled by a small horse. Mary Elizabeth liked this carriage for rural excursions, as it was easy to access for women wearing full skirts. By contrast, the two-wheeled American Buggy of around 1890 was very fast and sporty, and weighed so little it could be lifted by two men. The buggy remained popular with eligible young gentlemen keen to 'cut a dash', even when cars took to the roads.

The Carriage-house

The Spider Phaeton of about 1880 was an elegant four-wheeled carriage for town use, and its name reflects the pared-down, almost skeletal structure of the undercarriage. The fashionable occupants were able to look down on other traffic, and so were known as 'high-fliers'. The luxurious Park Barouche of about 1870 is the grandest carriage here, having cost 280 guineas, worth some £60,000 today. The liveried coachman drove a 'matching pair' of horses, with the footman in attendance. The Barouche was used by the Lucy family for the London Season, and carried four passengers in comfort. All the carriage furniture is silver-plated, and it has no external lamp holders, as the premier streets of Mayfair and Belgravia were now gaslit. For informal town trips, the Lucys used the Brougham, a closed carriage with room for four. Back at Charlecote, the Wagonette Omnibus was a versatile vehicle which could transport ten passengers. In summer, the Omnibus's upper section was removed using the hoist in the Carriage-house ceiling, to convert it into an 'open-top'.

Left The luxurious interior of the Park Barouche, c.1870

Below The Spider Phaeton, c.1880

The Garden
and Park

When the mansion was built in the 1550s, the Charlecote estate lay at the southern edge of the ancient forest of Arden.

Over time, the landscape became more open, as trees were removed to create a fashionable deer-park, enclosed by distinctive split-oak palings. The first Sir Thomas Lucy is believed to have planted the great double avenue of lime trees which still stretch from the house to the south-west, and his descendants were similarly keen to cultivate the setting.

Formal water

The River Avon and its tributary, the Dene, naturally divide the estate into three, and the waterways were used to aesthetic effect by the family. In the 1670s Captain Thomas Lucy (c.1655–84) instigated a formal water garden in the Dutch style to the north of the house. He began constructing *parterres,* geometrically laid-out flower beds, bordered by box hedges and separated by gravelled paths. Other innovations included a pair of large brick-lined ponds in which to breed carp, a strawberry house and an orangery complete with '4 apricock trees and 2 orin022 ', which cost 8s 4d. After Captain Thomas's early death, his cousin and heir, Colonel George Lucy, completed the garden, as it appears in the 'bird's-eye-view' painting of the late seventeenth century. At this stage, two canals ran north from the house, and in the octagonal brick-built gazebo at their

confluence, people would dine in summer, or fish from the windows in winter. Formal *parterres* alongside the canals sported box trees trimmed alternately into the shapes of cones or spheres. Two decorative *parterres* lay between the west front and the steps down to the river, and there was a walled kitchen garden in the angle where the Dene flowed into the Avon, where vegetables grew in serried ranks. Tree-lined avenues stretched to the east and west of the house, and a separate avenue ran diagonally across the park to St Leonard's church.

Though the height of sophistication at their creation, by the middle of the eighteenth century the Dutch-influenced formal gardens and the wider park at Charlecote seemed very outmoded, and 'Bachelor George' Lucy resolved to have the landscape remodelled by an emerging new talent, known as 'Capability' Brown.

Above The park and garden from the east in 1722

Opposite Late seventeenth-century bird's-eye view of the formal garden from the west

'Capability' Brown and the new Charlecote landscape

Above 'Capability' Brown, who transformed the parkland at Charlecote

Opposite The River Dene in autumn

Lancelot 'Capability' Brown (1716–83) was one of history's greatest landscape designers, as well as being a self-made entrepreneur and accomplished salesman.

Brown's nickname derived from his appealing ability to see great 'capabilities' for improvement in his wealthy clients' country estates. His naturalistic designs incorporated limpid lakes, rolling slopes, artfully grouped clumps of trees and strategically-placed picturesque follies. The result concealed the vast amount of effort, manpower and money expended to create the quintessential parkscape. It looked rather like the British countryside, but subtly better.

Packington and Charlecote

Brown's first recorded visit to Charlecote was in September 1757, but in 1759 he was asked to advise on the garden at Packington, about 20 miles away. It appears he also visited Charlecote at the same time, as a rough outline of this house and garden survives on the back of one of his Packington designs. In the following decade 'Bachelor George' Lucy was keen to improve the parkland. He had had a new humped-back bridge built across the Dene in 1755–7 by David Hiorne, who was also working at Packington with Brown. George recalled the landscape gardener and commissioned him to create a new cascade where the Dene joined the Avon, for which he was paid £36; this was later altered.

A grander commission

In 1760 Lucy gave 'Capability' Brown a much larger commission, requiring him to widen the River Avon and probably to sink the fosse (or ha-ha) around the meadow to keep out the deer. In addition, he modified the course of the Dene, as it ran too close to the house and needed rerouting into a more serpentine curve. Brown was also instructed to fill in the ponds on the north side of the house, to alter the contours of the slopes and to give the whole 'a natural, easy and corresponding level with the house on every side'.

Once the unfashionable water garden had been filled in, Brown created a raised lawn and planted it with cedars of Lebanon, still to be seen today. From this vantage point there are fine views along the Ladies Walk and across the surrounding gardens. The physical work was overseen by Brown's foreman, John Midgely, and cost a total of £525, which was paid in instalments. Brown was notably informal about payment; in April 1761, 'Bachelor George' ran into 'Capability' Brown in Bath. The client recalled: 'I told him the time was elapsed for a second payment, which he said was no matter as he did not want money, but upon my offering him a £100 note he pulled out his pocket book and carried it off with him'.

The gardens

Above The floral parterre

It was Mary Elizabeth Lucy whose Victorian sensibilities transformed the gardens and brought flowering plants close to the house once again.

A keen gardener, she was often in the grounds by 6 am on summer mornings, supervising the creation of new parterres between the two wings of the east front, and to the west, leading down to the River Avon (where her planting scheme was carefully reinstated in 1995).

A sunken croquet lawn provided the family and their guests of all ages the chance for fun outdoors on summer afternoons. To the north lies the Wilderness, planted by 'Capability' Brown with Scots pine and sculpted hedges of box and yew. On her arrival at Charlecote as a new bride, Mary Elizabeth was horrified to find it waist-deep in nettles. She ordered the dense undergrowth removed, and the planting of Solomon's seal, foxgloves, ivy, box and wild flowers.

The Orangery

Not content with horticulture alone, in 1857 Mary Elizabeth replaced her husband's Grecian-style summerhouse with a substantial and impressive orangery, which is now the restaurant. The building was designed by John Gibson, who was also responsible for the ornate entrance gates and the lodge. Orangeries were essential fixtures on many country estates houses. By the middle of the nineteenth century, ornamental and exotic plants were brought to Britain from all over the world and cultivated to meet the demands of avid Victorian collectors.

Decorative rarities, such as orchids, were initially planted and nurtured in hot-houses, and teams of gardeners ensured that the more delicate mature plants survived the winter months in purpose-built orangeries.

The Summer-house

The quaint thatched summer-house near the Orangery was put up by Mary Elizabeth, and was inspired by a visit she made as a child to meet the famous 'Ladies of Llangollen', Lady Eleanor Butler and Miss Sara Ponsonby, who lived together in an exquisite cottage. Rustic in appearance, the Charlecote Summer-house was furnished with child-sized tables and chairs, to amuse the Lucy children and grandchildren.

The Long Border close by has a mixed planting scheme providing plenty of seasonal interest from April to October.

The Mulberry Lawn

The Mulberry Lawn boasts some rarities; two *Morus nigra* (black mulberry trees) and a younger *Morus alba* (white mulberry). The eighteenth-century ha-ha installed by 'Capability' Brown still surrounds this section of the garden. This continuous steep-sided grassy ditch keeps questing and hungry deer out of the gardens, without imposing an intrusive barrier which would spoil the visual effect of an open, continuous landscape.

Left The Orangery

The Wider Estate

Fallow deer have been kept at Charlecote since the mid-1400s, and nowadays the herd numbers about 160 animals.

The deer can usually be seen amongst the trees which run along the Main Drive, and in the West Park, which is accessible on foot over the hump-backed bridge, and offers enjoyable walks 364 days a year. There is a public right of way in West Park, but dog walkers are required to keep their pets under control because of the livestock and wildlife.

Charlecote Park is bounded by distinctive hand-split wooden fences, made of rustic-looking upright palings of varying heights.

This centuries-old traditional design deters deer from jumping the barrier, as they find the irregularity of the uprights visually confusing. The ha-ha keeps them away from the gardens, and deer booms on the Dene and River Avon stop them swimming to escape. Deer normally socialise with their own gender, the does in one group and the bucks elsewhere, but in autumn the bucks compete to mate with the females, and the 'rut' is noisy and leads to clashing antlers. Their survival relies on their wariness of humans and other potential predators, so the Deer Sanctuary is closed to visitors to provide a refuge for the animals. Does with young fawns leave them concealed in the undergrowth while they feed. To ensure the continued health and welfare of the herd, the deer are managed by specialist staff, with an annual cull of any ailing or very old stock. Targetted animals are shot in the open air, to save them the stress associated with capture and transport. All deer products are used where possible, from the venison which is sold through the shop, to the antlers discarded naturally every year.

The Deer Sanctuary contains some magnificent ancient trees, including the Boundary Oak, which is more than 560 years old. The oaks are home to a substantial heronry, and owl boxes accommodate nesting barn owls. The waters of the Dene and the River Avon provide a habitat for swans and kingfishers, and there are more than 100 different species of bird at Charlecote. These nature reserves were once

home to humans too. An archaeological survey at a spot named Old Town Wood recently detected four substantial structures below the surface, possibly the remains of towers from a fort. It is known that there was a medieval village in West Park, where traces of ridge and furrow strip-farming are still visible. In the Middle Ages, each smallholder would manage a few strips of land, giving 25% of the crop to the landlord as their annual rent.

Opposite Bucks locking antlers

Left Charlecote's distinctive hand-split wooden fencing

Above The River Dene on a winter morning

Jacob sheep

The distinctive black and white Jacob Sheep at Charlecote are descendants of the first flock to be introduced to Britain.

It was 'Bachelor George' Lucy who encountered them in Portugal while visiting his friend, the British Ambassador to Lisbon, and he had a number of them shipped to England in 1756. The Charlecote flock remains one of the most numerous in the country, with about 80 ewes and usually three resident rams. Jacob sheep are a hardy breed, but are not often bred commercially because they are naturally lean, and so their meat yield is low compared with other breeds. Each fully-grown ewe weighs about 65–70 kilos, while a mature rams weighs about 100 kilos, and requires careful management, as they are inclined to be energetic and boisterous. The flock receives extra feed supplements to keep them healthy, and they are fond of licking the stonework of bridges on the estate for the mineral content.

The ewes are known for being particularly good mothers, mostly producing single lambs, though occasionally they give birth to twins. The flock usually inhabit the Polo Field, which is split into seven smaller paddocks including a lambing shed. Lambing time in Spring is particularly popular with visitors.

Trees

The parkland at Charlecote is dotted with a wide variety of trees, and their care and maintenance is an important aspect of the property staff's work. The Lime Avenue of venerable trees requires regular monitoring for infestation, deadwood or damage, and there are plans to reinstate the historic feature as it existed in previous centuries. The trees nearest the house are 300 years old, while those further away are approx 200 years old, and the avenue is one of the oldest and longest in England. The trees were planted along what used to be the main public thoroughfare to nearby Wellesbourne, but the road was re-routed around the estate, and now West Lodge Gate marks the outer boundary of Charlecote Park.

Since 2005, the estate team at Charlecote have planted more than 130 trees, largely along the property boundaries, but also to replace natural casualties inside the park. Natural England have also funded a Higher Level Stewardship Partnership Scheme, funding a major programme of tree-planting through the provision of a grant. Saplings planted are mostly oaks, alders, sweet chestnuts and black poplars.

The natural ecological cycle is sensitively managed. When trees die, their remains are deliberately left to decay naturally, as they provide valuable habitats and food supplies for invertebrates. The cultivated trees are also popular with Charlecote's livestock; the apples and pears produced by the trees in the orchard are often eaten by fallow deer.

Opposite Jacob sheep

Left Fallen trees provide a rich habitat for rare invertebrates

Below The park on a frosty morning

A home for wildlife

provide food for the household, and so needs occasional dredging for maintenance. The red and purple blooms of the flowering rush, which flourishes at one end of the lake, attract butterflies and dragonflies, though the plant is so vigorous it needs regular cutting back to keep it in check. Newts also thrive in the vegetation around the water's edge.

Hill Park on the far side of the lake has a historic flour mill, and there are a number of striking 'ghost trees', which have come to the end of their natural lives, but remain upright and are left on site as they are an important part of the local ecology, providing habitats and food for

The wider parkland to the north and east of the house is home to a huge variety of wildlife.

The Front Park is populated by small groups of fallow deer who use the dappled shade thrown by trees as shelter and camouflage, hence their spotted markings. The footpath towards the lake passes the site of another abandoned settlement, probably medieval, and there is a one-way entrance gate to the churchyard of St Leonard's. A spinney provides valuable dense cover for small birds.

The lake is a haven for waterfowl, especially Canada Geese, and swans nest on the island. It is quite shallow, because it was artificially created in the late seventeenth century as fishponds to

invertebrates. There are also elegant cedars, whose spreading branches are prone to accumulate weighty layers of snow in the winter, and evergreen turkey oaks. All timber collected from the parkland at Charlecote is collected to be used as firewood in the Victorian kitchen. Places Meadow lies in the flood plain of the River Avon, a stretch of particularly verdant pasture dotted with buttercups, and is spectacular when its wildflowers bloom. The National Trust recently planted more than 9,000 plug plants in this meadow, native wildflower species such as ox-eye daisies and red burnett. The British Trust for Ornithology regularly monitors the birdlife in this part of the estate, ringing swallows and conducting owl surveys. Places Meadow and the adjacent cricket pitch are popular with birdwatchers for the opportunities to see kingfishers, and barbell, chubb, tench and pike inhabit the River Avon.

Across the river lies Camp Ground; during the Civil War, Oliver Cromwell's army camped there before the Battle of Edgehill. It is also part of the Charlecote estate, and abuts the Deer Sanctuary, but it is not accessible to visitors. Camp Ground is managed as a valuable nature reserve, as it attracts wildfowl and is a haven for goldfinches and butterflies.

Opposite above Ox-eye daisies are among the wildflowers that flourish on Places Meadow

Opposite below Kingfisher

Above Goldfinch

St Leonard's Church

The church of St Leonard's was first built around 1187, when Cecily de Lucie gave land to be used as a burial ground.

The original structure comprised a nave with boxed pews, and a wooden gallery above. At the east end was the altar, a family pew and the family crypt. There were two porches, one for the sole use of the Lucy family, the other for the parishioners. The Reverend Richard Southam was the vicar in Shakespeare's time; in 1585, he wrote gloomily 'Our parisshe is but small, it is but seaven howsis besides the manor house of Sir Thomas Lucy Knighte … [who] is patron of the vicarage of Charlcott, there is no glebe lands belonging to the viccaridge. I have no other benefice….'

Mary Elizabeth Lucy had the old church demolished in 1849, and a larger one rebuilt by John Gibson in 1850, in memory of her late husband George. The three grandest Lucy family monuments, which date from the late sixteenth and seventeenth centuries, were moved from the old chancel to the Victorian Lucy Chapel. The alabaster tomb on the right-hand side of the Chapel was erected by the first Sir Thomas Lucy in memory of his wife Joyce, who died in 1595. The figure of Sir Thomas was added after his own death in 1600.

Left St Leonard's church,
Charlecote

In 1890, the body of Mary Elizabeth, the creator of St Leonard's, was interred in the family crypt. Many other members of the family are commemorated on plaques around the walls, including Sir Brian Fulke Fairfax-Lucy, 5th Baronet (1898–1974). His brother, the 4th Baronet, Sir Henry Montgomerie Fairfax-Lucy (1896–1965), gave Charlecote Park to the National Trust in 1946; it had been in his family since the twelfth century.

Opposite is the magnificent monument to his son, the second Sir Thomas Lucy. This unusual design was carved from alabaster, marble and oolite. He had two wives, and died in 1605. The 14 children of the two marriages are depicted on the front panel. The knight in armour has his crest at his feet, and a lifelike figure of his second wife, Constance, kneels in prayer alongside the tomb. The most impressive monument, in black and white Carrara marble, commemorates the third Sir Thomas Lucy, who died in 1640, after a fall from his horse. The monument had been attributed to Bernini, the celebrated Italian sculptor, but it is now known that Schurman, who assisted the well-known sculptor Nicholas Stone, was responsible for most of the monument.

The Lucys of Charlecote

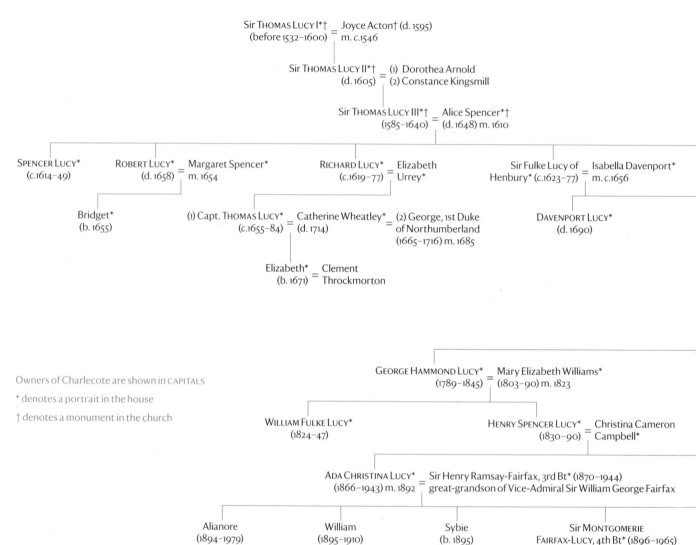

Sir THOMAS LUCY I*† = Joyce Acton† (d. 1595)
(before 1532–1600)   m. c.1546

Sir THOMAS LUCY II*† = (1) Dorothea Arnold
(d. 1605)   (2) Constance Kingsmill

Sir THOMAS LUCY III*† = Alice Spencer*†
(1585–1640)   (d. 1648) m. 1610

SPENCER LUCY*   ROBERT LUCY* = Margaret Spencer*   RICHARD LUCY* = Elizabeth   Sir Fulke Lucy of = Isabella Davenport*
(c.1614–49)   (d. 1658)   m. 1654   (c.1619–77)   Urrey*   Henbury* (c.1623–77)   m. c.1656

Bridget*   (1) Capt. THOMAS LUCY* = Catherine Wheatley* = (2) George, 1st Duke   DAVENPORT LUCY*
(b. 1655)   (c.1655–84)   (d. 1714)   of Northumberland   (d. 1690)
                                                (1665–1716) m. 1685

Elizabeth* = Clement
(b. 1671)   Throckmorton

Owners of Charlecote are shown in CAPITALS

* denotes a portrait in the house

† denotes a monument in the church

GEORGE HAMMOND LUCY* = Mary Elizabeth Williams*
(1789–1845)   (1803–90) m. 1823

WILLIAM FULKE LUCY*   HENRY SPENCER LUCY* = Christina Cameron
(1824–47)   (1830–90)   Campbell*

ADA CHRISTINA LUCY* = Sir Henry Ramsay-Fairfax, 3rd Bt* (1870–1944)
(1866–1943) m. 1892   great-grandson of Vice-Admiral Sir William George Fairfax

Alianore   William   Sybie   Sir MONTGOMERIE
(1894–1979)   (1895–1910)   (b. 1895)   FAIRFAX-LUCY, 4th Bt* (1896–1965)

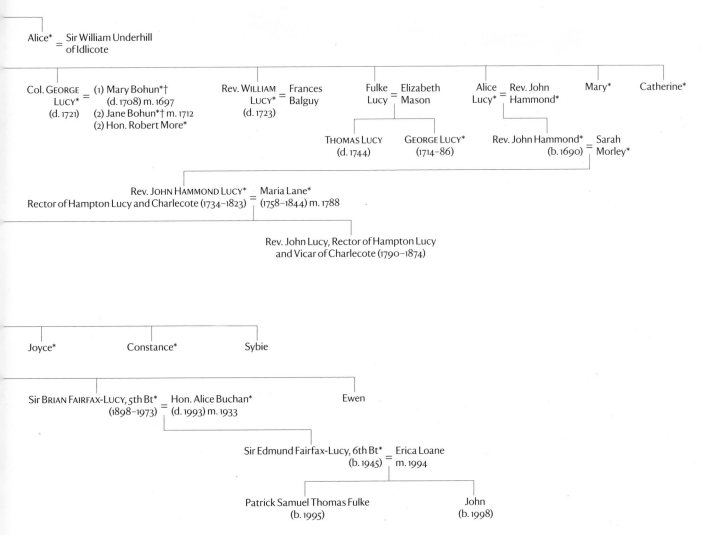

Alice* = Sir William Underhill of Idlicote

Col. GEORGE LUCY* (d. 1721) = (1) Mary Bohun*† (d. 1708) m. 1697 (2) Jane Bohun*† m. 1712 (2) Hon. Robert More*

Rev. WILLIAM LUCY* (d. 1723) = Frances Balguy

Fulke Lucy = Elizabeth Mason

Alice Lucy* = Rev. John Hammond*

Mary*

Catherine*

THOMAS LUCY (d. 1744)

GEORGE LUCY* (1714–86)

Rev. John Hammond* (b. 1690) = Sarah Morley*

Rev. JOHN HAMMOND LUCY* Rector of Hampton Lucy and Charlecote (1734–1823) = Maria Lane* (1758–1844) m. 1788

Rev. John Lucy, Rector of Hampton Lucy and Vicar of Charlecote (1790–1874)

Joyce*

Constance*

Sybie

Sir BRIAN FAIRFAX-LUCY, 5th Bt* (1898–1973) = Hon. Alice Buchan* (d. 1993) m. 1933

Ewen

Sir Edmund Fairfax-Lucy, 6th Bt* (b. 1945) = Erica Loane m. 1994

Patrick Samuel Thomas Fulke (b. 1995)

John (b. 1998)

The children of
Thomas Lucy III